Deputising a high school principal, Chain Mkhawana left the Education Department, hoping to join the corporate world in 2007. His hope was overhauled when the Holy Spirit enrolled him for the subject, Jesus Christ, the Saviour of the world until the end of 2010. After these spiritual classes, he began writing and became an English lecturer at a TVET college. He had majored in English for his STD at Tivumbeni College of Education and at UNISA for his bachelor degree. Chain Mkhawana had also taught high school English drama and poetry for 17 years. Writing Christian books fulfils him more than all the things he does.

Chain Chayintonga Mkhawana

SHALL I NOT DRINK THE CUP THE FATHER HAS GIVEN ME

AUSTIN MACAULEY PUBLISHERS™
LONDON • CAMBRIDGE • NEW YORK • SHARJAH

Copyright © Chain Chayintonga Mkhawana 2024

The right of Chain Chayintonga Mkhawana to be identified as author of this work has been asserted by the author in accordance with sections 77 and 78 of the Copyright, Designs and Patents Act 1988.

All rights reserved. No part of this publication may be reproduced, stored in a retrieval system or transmitted in any form or by any means, electronic, mechanical, photocopying, recording or otherwise, without the prior permission of the publishers.

Any person who commits any unauthorised act in relation to this publication may be liable to criminal prosecution and civil claims for damages.

A CIP catalogue record for this title is available from the British Library.

ISBN 9781788489959 (Paperback)
ISBN 9781788788939 (Hardback)
ISBN 9781788788946 (ePub e-book)

www.austinmacauley.com

First Published 2024
Austin Macauley Publishers Ltd®
1 Canada Square
Canary Wharf
London
E14 5AA

The Lord prodded me to start writing this book weeks before a stroke struck me. Healing at Muel-Med Rehab, I perceived that this book is a voice of the Lord: Anyone who hears the voice crosses over from death to life. The book is therefore dedicated to the Lord, to Christian who has already crossed over and to people who are willing to hear the voice.

I came to Austin Macauley Publishers after a publisher had offered to publish *Judah Game Reserve,* my first book. Something prompted me to find another publisher. I came to AMP who found *Judah Game Reserve* not good for any market. Then I concluded that Austin Macauley Publishers' editors can turn me into a good author. I sent them *Shall I not drink The cup The Father Has Given me?* AMP, I look forward to becoming your great pupil, and a good teacher to readers. However, I acknowledge more than it is the Lord God's mind that I am allowed to reap in the name of the Lord Jesus Christ.

Table of Contents

Synopsis	11
Pencilled In Impish Glee	14
We Are a Vineyard of the Lord God	18
A Cup of Salvation	22
Destined for the Universe	28
Smoothing the Sojourn's Messiness	32
In Eternal Cyclic Existence	39
The Rising Day of Selflessness	42
Boanerges' Request Reworded	47
At the Name of Jesus	50
Quo Vadis?	57

Synopsis

The titles of this book, the epiplexis and the command, are responses to Apostle Peter's attempt to lock the Lord Jesus Christ away in Israel far from the universe, where he is destined. The nine rhyming couplets below are a skeleton of the book.

> Shall I not drink the cup the Father has given me?
> Satan's face will light up with pencilled in impish glee.
> This cup of all sinners' sinfulness I will drink, die,
> resurrect, and then to the universe fly.
> Except daughters and sons of perdition,
> My disciples will all each have a cup of Salvation.
> Destined for the unimaginably huge universe,
> In Israel, I sojourned until this mess.
> Satan has never matched the unmatched Archangel Michael;
> Now his followers will follow me out of his eternal vicious cycle.
> Have your sword go with the setting day of selfishness;
> I am your rising day of selflessness.
> My Lordship by every tongue will forever be confessed;
> In bowing to me all knees enmeshed.

The world will at last be a philanthropic club.
If two or more soon drink from the very cup.
So you will not be my stumbling block, Peter;
Your horizon the Father will widen wider.

The Lord rhetorically asked, "Shall I not drink the cup the Father has given me?" He asked the question to make a point rather than to get an answer. Like William Shakespeare's "Shall I compare thee to a summer's day?" the Lord Jesus Christ's "Shall I not drink the cup the Father has given me?" is an epiplexis, a specific kind of rhetorical question in which a lament or an insult is asked, mainly to upbraid or reproach, but not to elicit information or answer. The point that a rhetorician makes by using a rhetorical question is the opposite of the question. In asking the positive epiplexis "Shall I compare thee to a summer's day?" Shakespeare successfully argued that the 'thee' in his sonnet had been beyond compare; whereas in asking the negative "Shall I not drink the cup the Father has given me?" the Lord Jesus Christ declared that nothing would stop him from drinking the cup. The Lord God had prepared the cup and had given it to his son to drink for the denouement of his first play and the prologue of his new play. Drinking the cup was meant to be the anti-climax of the Lord God's first play, and unless the cup was drunk the Lord God's new play would be without a prologue.

"Shall I not drink the cup the Father has given me? Put your sword back in its place!"

Mkhawana Chain.

Pencilled In Impish Glee

Shall I not drink the cup the Father has given me?
Satan's face will light up with pencilled in impish glee.

The German *schadenfreude* and the English *epicaricacy* are slight synonyms for *impish glee*, meaning to rejoice or derive pleasure from the misfortunes of others. The Lord God knew from time immemorial that Satan's face would light up with impish glee when the Lord Jesus Christ would be led to Calvary. He knows that Satan's great delight always comes from the misfortunes of others. He therefore pencilled in an impish glee as a cup for anyone who could crucify the Lord Jesus Christ. Not seeing that the impish glee had not been inked in yet, and that the cup had been overdosed with worry, Satan gave in to crucifying the Lord. He drank the cup of pencilled in impish glee overdosed with worry. The Lord God erased the pencil drawing instead of inking it in. The Lord Jesus Christ rose from the dead, ascended to heaven and sent down here the Holy Spirit who makes him omnipresent, and then Satan uncovered that it had been a cup of endless despondency and melancholy that he had drunk. That is how the Lord God outwits Satan. The pencilled in impish glee is a flourishing fisher of arrogant wicked people who look at the Lord's fishers of men with contempt. Satan and his arrogant wicked people are fish. The Lord God uses pencilled in impish glee as bait to lure them out of water. Lured out of water with pencilled in impish glee they live dead forever, but lured out with the Lord God's word we live alive forever.

For pencilled in impish glee to work perfectly well victimised people must put away their swords of selfishness and take up the Lord Jesus Christ's sword of selflessness. "Do you think I cannot call on my Father and he will at once put at my disposal more than twelve legions of angels?" In the presence of a Jewish-soldier detachment that had been sent to arrest the Lord Jesus Christ, the Lord himself asked Apostle Peter the epiplexis (Matthew 26:53). The Lord asked it secondarily to upbraid the apostle, who in an attempt to be his bodyguard had just cut off Malchus' ear, and to inform the soldiers that his bodyguards were twelve invisible legions of angels. Primarily, he asked it to make the point that he chose not to let the best defence in the universe defend him against the arrest. People send soldiers to fight for them in battles, the Lord God angels. Can soldiers stand against angels? The Lord rhetorically asked, "Shall I not drink the cup the Father has given me?" If he had not been firmly resolute to drink the bitter cup of all sinners' sinfulness, he would have chosen to let the universe's best defence defend him. He chose to drink the cup not because he had been defenceless, but because he like the Father wanted for our sake Satan's face to light up with pencilled in impish glee. When the soldiers told him that they wanted a man called Jesus of Nazareth, he answered, "I am he," (John 18:6) and then the soldiers, carrying weapons, drew back and fell to the ground. What 'I am he' is this that pushed armed soldiers back to fall to the ground? Who else in all the history of the world has ever uttered such an 'I am he'?

The Lord's 'I am he' is deadlier than fire-carrying soldiers. Could the soldiers who drew back and fell to the ground at hearing the Lord's 'I am he' stand against twelve invisible legions of angels? It is the Lord God who crucified the Lord Jesus Christ, or else the Lord Jesus Christ crucified himself. The Lord's 'I am he', without the twelve invisible legions of angels, is deadlier than fire-carrying soldiers. There were the soldiers who had been sent to arrest the Lord, drawn back from him and down to the ground. His 'I am he' had made them too doddery to arrest him. Was he crucified because he was unable to kill his crucifiers, Satan and the Sanhedrin? Killing Satan and his agents is worthless because another Satan and other agents can be up for opposition a twinkle of an eye after the killing. Throwing them into Hell is the best option to punish them. Making their faces light up with pencilled in impish glee here consumes their souls like the fire that consumes souls in Hell. There were the soldiers who had been sent to arrest the Lord, drawn back from him and down to the ground. His 'I am he' had not killed but made them too doddery to arrest him. Their next possible move could be to report to the chief priests, teachers of law and elders that when they advanced to arrest the Lord his 'I am he' drew them back and down to the ground. Is it not sometimes rather better to be killed than humiliated? What cheerless smiles of anger the report would still be arousing! It could still be chanted that Jewish soldiers are trained neither to fight nor to kill, but to draw back from the enemy and fall to the ground, and it could still be sung that Jewish soldiers were once physically overpowered by the Lord Jesus Christ. There were the soldiers who had been sent to arrest the Lord, drawn back from him and down to the ground. His 'I am he' had not killed, but made them too doddery to arrest him. However, he knew that showing the world how greatly glorified he had been to defend himself would thwart the Lord God's divine plan to have Satan's face light up with pencilled in impish glee. How would the Scriptures be fulfilled (Matthew 26:54) if he defeated the ends of the Crucifixion? The Scriptures are the heart of the Lord God. The Lord Jesus Christ had declared at Gethsemane that whether he should be crucified or not had been the Lord God's will (Matthew 26:39). He had thus acknowledged that he had been born to live by the book, the Scriptures that had been written about him many centuries earlier. Like a lamb to a slaughter, and as a sheep before its shearers is silent, he did not open his mouth when led to Calvary (Isaiah 53:7). He is not the Pig of God, but the Lamb of God who takes away the sin of the world. A Pig of God would have oinked, snorted, squealed, and grunted all the way to Golgotha, imploring the Father to make the world hundred percent piggish and priggish. Satan's face would forever light up with inked in impish glee. There were the soldiers who had been sent to arrest the Lord, drawn back from him and down to the ground. His 'I am he' had not killed but made them too doddery to arrest him. Formidably with self-defence, the Lord God had armed the Lord so that the Crucifixion would not be a result of helplessness. In the Lord God's first play, Satan's face nearly always lighted with inked in impish glee because *I am He* was not there yet. Anyone in the Lord God's new plan can make evildoers too doddery to touch them because *I am He* is here. At last, the Lord let the soldiers arrest him on condition that they let his disciples go untouched (John 18:8).

We Are a Vineyard of the Lord God

This cup of all sinners' sinfulness I will drink, die, resurrect, and then to the universe fly.

Centuries before the Lord Jesus Christ had asked his epiplexis the Lord God had asked his (Isaiah 5:4): "What more could have been done for my vineyard than I have done for it? This epiplexis is the basis for the explanation of the metaphorical phrase 'drink the cup'. The Lord God compares the human race to his vineyard on a fertile hillside (Isaiah 5:1). We are his vineyard: *He ploughs us, clears us of stones, plants us with the choicest vines, builds a watchtower and cuts a winepress within us, and looks then* for a *crop of good grapes, but receives only a yield of bitter grapes* (Isaiah 5:2). In spite of all the plenteous, quality offers the Lord God makes to settle us in environments conducive to righteousness we remain unrighteous. Consequently, with the very winepress he cut within us he presses the very bitter grapes we produce to have us each has a cup of our own bitter grapes. We infer from Isaiah 5:5–6 how bitter this cup of our own unrighteousness is: The Lord God breaks down the vineyard wall so that the vineyard is exposed to tramplers and annihilators; he neither prunes nor cultivates it anymore so that it becomes a wasteland and he commands clouds never to rain on it anymore. The cup of our own unrighteousness is the bitterest of all cups. We are a vineyard of the Lord God. Our own skilled people are the choicest vines the Lord God plants us with. From the watchtower, he built within us we see enemies coming our way a long distance away and pre-empt them, and our social evaluation systems are the winepress he has cut within us. Somebody can neither be married nor hired for a job because pressed in the winepress they come out too bitter to be drunk."

The cup of our own unrighteousness is the bitterest of all. When the Lord God asked about the whereabouts of Abel Cain asked an erotisis (Genesis 4:9): "Am I my brother's keeper?" An erotisis is a rhetorical question asked in confident expectation of a negative answer. Ready for a verbal fight, Cain asked the erotisis when asked where the Abel he had killed had been. However, he pleaded for mitigation when the Lord God gave him to drink the cup of murdering Abel, "My punishment is more than I can bear. Today you are driving me from the land, and I will be hidden from your presence; I will be a restless wanderer on the earth, and whoever finds me will kill me." The cup of our own unrighteousness is the bitterest of all? Hours before Cain had murdered Abel, he had seen the act of drinking the cup of his evil turn his sweet sorrow into bitter sorrow, his sweet warm day into a bitter cold night. Nevertheless, he still did the evil deed, asked the erotisis, and then seeing that his cold night could be longer than his life he pleaded for mitigation. Who could on Cain's day, 6021 years ago, drink another person's cup of unrighteousness? The Lord God had not established yet the institute of altruism in the world. Consequently, Cain left the presence of the Lord God for Nod, a land home to restless wanderers. For millennia, people died in thousands in Nod until Jesus Christ the Institute of Altruism drank on our behalf the bitterest cup of our own unrighteousness.

Shall we continue drinking the bitterest cup of our own unrighteousness that the Lord drank more than two millennia ago? Let us see what happened of Saul to understand the paradox of the Lord God's grace (1 Corinthians 15:5–10): The Lord Jesus Christ drank the cup of all sinners' sinfulness, appeared to many, and then at last to Saul too as to one abnormally born. Saul then acknowledged that though he had been the least of the apostles, and undeserving to be called an apostle because he had persecuted Christians, the Lord God's grace had paradoxically made him work harder than all the normally born apostles. Grace in the Lord God's new play is manifested in saving repentant sinners. As like charges the grace of the Lord God and trusting only in the sweat of our brows (Genesis 3:19) repel from each other. Shall we continue drinking the bitterest cup of our own unrighteousness that the Lord drank more than two millennia ago? The last after the Judgment Day will be eternally drunk as faithful brides of Jesus Christ the Bridegroom will be eternally drinking that of the eternal banquet bliss. "Truly I tell you, I do not know you," Jesus Christ the Bridegroom will on the Judgment Day say to the billions of foolish virgins glowing without the Holy Spirit today (Matthew 25:12). The word lamps as used in the Parable of the Ten Virgins, refers to human hearts, oil to the Holy Spirit. In their lifetime, foolish virgins trim their lamps every time wise virgins trim theirs (Matthew 25:7). It is surprising that even those who are totally averse to buying oil do trim their lamps. Foolish virgins have without the Holy

Spirit a way of looking more Christian than wise virgins. Wise virgins will have an eternal wedding banquet after the Judgment Day. Shortly before the Judgment Day, while foolish virgins will be away to buy the Holy Spirit, wise virgins will go in with Jesus Christ the Bridegroom to the eternal wedding banquet and the door will be shut (Matthew 25:10). Foolish virgins will return later and ask the Lord to open the door for them. "Truly I tell you, I do not know you," the Lord will say this to lock them out of eternal banquet bliss. The time to buy the Holy Spirit, become a faithful bride, and then be known by Jesus Christ the Bridegroom is now. If anyone does not let the Lord Jesus Christ drink the cup of their own unrighteousness today, they will on their own eternally drink the worst after the Judgment Day.

A Cup of Salvation

Except sons and daughters of perdition,
My disciples will all each have a cup of Salvation.

Like Spicy Pork Vindaloo is a main dish, cheesecake a dessert, Jesus Christ the Word of God is a main dish, a cup of Salvation a dessert. "Shall I not drink the cup the Father has given me?" the Lord asked at the time when his disciples had long been served the appetiser by John the Baptist and the main dish by himself. The dessert had not been served yet. The Lord Jesus Christ was at the Crucifixion dressed in a robe dipped in his own blood (Revelation 19:13), and then after the Resurrection, he breathed the Holy Spirit on his disciples (John 20:22), serving the dessert, a cup of Salvation. Hardly fifty days before the Lord's disciples had drunk the cup of Salvation, Judas Iscariot plunged head over heels into Hell. The Lord was dressed in the robe dipped in his own blood, that is to say he was made to drink the cup of all sinners' sinfulness, resurrected on the third day, and then hardly fifty days after Judas Iscariot had plunged head over heels into Hell he breathed the Holy Spirit on the disciples, serving the dessert, the cup of Salvation. Judas Iscariot, the son of perdition, did not drink the dessert, the cup of Salvation. In drinking the bitterest cup of our unrighteousness, the Lord prepared the cup of Salvation for us all except for daughters and sons of perdition. The Lord said that while he had been with his disciples he had protected and kept them safe by the name the Lord God had given him, and therefore none except Judas Iscariot the son of perdition had been lost (John 17:12). Jesus Christ the Word of God (Revelation 19:13), or Jesus Christ the Bread of Life (John 6:35), or Jesus Christ the Food that Endures to Eternal Life (John 6:27) is the name by which the Lord Jesus Christ had protected and kept his disciples safe for three years until they each drank the dessert, the cup of Salvation. Right from the beginning of the Lord's three-year corporeal ministry, Judas Iscariot had chosen not to be protected and kept safe by the name. The Lord shielded, every single day of the three years, all his disciples with the name, and Judas Iscariot, every single day of the three years, took off the Lord's shield to put on his. No wonder it is said he had been a thief who used to help himself to the money in the bag he was assigned to keep ((John 12:6). For three years, he daily took off Jesus Christ the Word of God to put on his no-use shield of life. That is how he had become the son of utter destruction. "Shall I not drink the cup the Father has given me?" the Lord Jesus Christ asked the epiplexis after three years of shielding his disciples with Jesus Christ the Word of God. Time for the dessert, the cup of Salvation, had come. Like Spicy Pork Vindaloo is a main dish, cheesecake a dessert, Jesus Christ the Word of God is a main dish, the cup of Salvation a dessert. In the spirit and power of Prophet Elijah, John the Baptist had long served the appetiser to the disciples and had been martyred. Jesus Christ the Word of God had also served himself already to them. The wedding banquet of the Lord Jesus Christ is given twenty-four seven and its three-course meal is not at all customisable. Mercedes-Benz does build any of their cars with our specifications if we have money, but the three-course meal in the wedding banquet of the Lord Jesus Christ is forever eaten unmodified. Christians who insist that it be customised for them never drink the dessert, the cup of Salvation. Jesus Christ the End of Law (Romans 10:4) says that until heaven and earth disappear, not the smallest letter, not the least stroke of a pen, will by any means disappear from the Law (Matthew 5:18). Judas Iscariot customised the main dish for himself to a lesser degree, but largely he simply ate only a little of John the Baptist's appetiser and of the Lord's main dish. Google reports that his parents were Sadducees and that when he joined John the Baptist's disciples the parents disowned him. In leaving the Sadducees to join John the Baptist group, he aggravated the holy war between the two groups: The Sadducees believed that there is no resurrection, and that there are neither angels nor spirits (Acts 23:8), but like the Pharisees, the John the Baptist group which heralded Christianity believed all the three things. It is said that Judas Iscariot's Sadducean friends influenced him more tremendously than anybody else. Sewer water had found a conduit to flow from Lake Death to Lake Life. With his one leg on Lake Life, his other left on Lake Death, Judas Iscariot became a victim of resentment. On Jesus Christ's triumphal entry into Jerusalem, a prominent member of Lake Death gleefully ridiculed him. "Why so troubled of countenance, my good friend, cheer up and join us all while we acclaim this Jesus of Nazareth the king of the Jews as he rides through the gates of Jerusalem seated on an ass." Like the Greeks and Romans, members of Lake Death looked down upon anyone who would consent to ride upon the ass or the colt of an ass because they were a party of high priests, aristocratic families and merchants. As king of the humble the Lord Jesus Christ consented to ride through Jerusalem gates seated on an ass' colt. Sewer water had found a conduit to flow from Lake Death to Lake Life. Knowing well that Lake Death's members did not believe in resurrection, Judas Iscariot anticipated further mockery against Lazarus' resurrection. The anticipation weighed heavily on him, adding to his resentment. His resentment fermented a day before the betrayal when the Lord rebuked him for thinking that Mary had wasted an expensive perfume by breaking it on his feet (John 12:7–8): "Leave her alone. It was intended that she should save this perfume for the day of my burial. You will always have the poor among you, but you will not always have me." Sewer water had found a conduit to flow from Lake Death to Lake Life. Jesus Christ the Word of God protected Mary from being given a cup of sewer water from Lake Death. The Lord knew that Judas Iscariot was the conduit, but he destroyed neither the conduit nor Lake Death. He knew that another Lake Death and another conduit would be established a twinkle of an eye after their destruction. Making their faces light up with pencilled in impish glee would kill them better. Indeed, the pencilled in impish glee did consume their souls like the fire that consumes souls in Hell: Judas Iscariot soon committed suicide, and the Sadducee group dissolved in 73 CE.

An agent of more abominations of desolation could have become of Judas Iscariot if he had not committed suicide. The suicide fulfilled the Scripture that said his days had to be few and his leadership office taken by another (Psalm 109:8). Daughters and sons of perdition are havens of Satan in houses of the Lord God, profaners of holy altars, agents of abominations that cause desolation. Betraying the Lord Jesus Christ is the abomination of desolation that Judas Iscariot committed. Scholars say that the first 'Son of Perdition' reference is to Antiochus IV Epiphanes, the king of Syria who captured Jerusalem in 167 BCE, desecrated the Second Temple by building a Zeus altar within it, and then sacrificed a swine on the altar. Sacrificing a swine on a Zeus altar in Yahweh's Temple is an abomination of desolation that Antiochus IV Epiphanes committed. Jezebel and her husband tore down Yahweh's altars, making Baal and Asherah national havens of Satan in Israel.

As long as spectators briskly flee to mountains when they see an abomination of desolation played, the abomination is a game that afflicts only its player. How gruesomely Jezebel, Antiochus IV Epiphanes and Judas Iscariot died! Thrown from a high window, Jezebel's unattended body was devoured by dogs (2 Kings 9:30–37); Antiochus IV Epiphanes heard that his army had been defeated in Judea, boarded a ship and fled to the coastal cities where wherever he came people rebelled and called him 'The Fugitive' until he drowned himself in the sea; filled with no repentance, but remorse for his betrayal of the Lord, Judas Iscariot fell so headlong that his body burst open, and all his intestines spilled out (Acts 1:18). In asking the negative epiplexis, "Shall I not drink the cup the Father has given me?" the Lord Jesus Christ declared that nothing would stop him from drinking the cup of our own unrighteousness, preparing the cup of Salvation for each of us except for daughters and sons of perdition.

The Lord Jesus Christ warns us to flee to the mountains when we see standing in holy places what the prophet Daniel called the abomination that causes desolation (Matthew 24:15). Fleeing from a desecrated holy place to mountains should not be seen as a result of faithlessness and fear, but of obedience and righteousness. There is no cup of Salvation in deliberately watching or revolting against an abomination of desolation. As long as spectators briskly flee to mountains when they see an abomination of desolation played, the abomination is a game that afflicts only its player. Jezebel had been born a Baal player, King Ahab her husband and the Israelites Yahweh-Worship players. The king and the Israelites did not flee to mountains when they saw Jezebel playing her abomination of desolation in Yahweh's Worship House. They instead spectated, became fanatic fans, and then played her game. King Ahab, therefore, was killed in Aram, and the Israelites were by King Hazael of Aram made to look like dust at threshing time. Seeing that an abomination of desolation is too catastrophic to be watched or revolted against, the Lord Jesus Christ drank the cup the Father had given him and ordered us to flee to the mountains as soon as it is seen. There is no cup of Salvation in deliberately watching or revolting against an abomination of desolation.

Destined for the Universe

Destined for the unimaginably huge universe.
In Israel, I sojourned until this mess.

Google defines the universe as everything we can touch, feel, sense, measure or detect, including living things, planets, stars, galaxies, dust clouds, light and even time. Let not the Bible fact that from Galilee the Lord ascended to heaven (Acts 1:11) make you think it is fallacious to say he had been destined to the Universe. Apostle Paul details the truth (Ephesians 4:10): "He who descended is the very one who ascended higher than all the heavens, in order to fill the whole universe." The coronation of Jesus Christ the King of the Universe began when he at Calvary said (John 19:30), "It is finished." When the Lord Jesus Christ died, he began to fill the position of kingship in the universe. He went under the earth, the place of shadows, pain, anguish, distress, darkness and hell. There he confiscated from Satan the keys of Death and Hell. So when it was thought the Lord had died he had been alive, confiscating from Satan the keys that made Satan think he had been God. He rose from the dead and said (Revelation 1:18), "Here are keys of death and Hades." The coronation was not over yet. At the Ascension, he ascended higher than all the heavens, in order to fill the whole universe.

Google defines the universe as everything we can touch, feel, sense, measure or detect, including living things, planets, stars, galaxies, dust clouds, light and even time. In defining the universe time, which is an abstract noun, is from a Christian point of view more useful than the concrete nouns (living things, planets, stars, galaxies, dust clouds and light) are The Lord God's word speaks of the universe in the past (Acts 14:16) and the universe these last days (Hebrews 1:1). "Shall I not drink the cup the Father has given me?" The Lord asked this epiplexis shortly before a turning point occurred: His drinking of the cup made the universe evolve from the universe of his first play into the one of his new play. The Lord God hid his secret wisdom from the universe in the past and revealed him to the universe these last days (1 Corinthians 2:7). In the past, he let all nations go their own way (Acts 14:16), but spoke to them through the prophets (Hebrews 1:1) and testified himself to them by giving them rain from heaven and crops in their seasons (Acts 14:17). In these last days, he speaks to us by his son, the Lord Jesus Christ (Hebrews 1:2). Should he speak to the universe by somebody else other than his son who drank the cup that brought forth the watershed? The CV of the son had already been the most excellent in the universe: He is the firstborn over all creation (Colossians 1:15); He had already been appointed heir of all things (Hebrews 1:2); Through him the universe had already been made (Hebrews 1:2); As the radiance of the Lord God's glory and the exact representation of the Lord God's being he had already been sustaining all things by his powerful word (Hebrews 1:3); After his provision of sins' purification he had already been seated at the right hand of the Majesty in heaven (Hebrews 1:3); All angels and servants of the Lord God had already been worshiping him because angels are spirits, servants flames of fire, but he sits on a throne (Hebrews 1:7).

The Lord God hid his secret wisdom from the universe in the past and revealed him to the universe these last days (1 Corinthians 2:7). His secret wisdom is the Holy Spirit. Before time had begun, said Apostle Paul (1 Corinthians 2:7), the Holy Spirit had been there, but as a gift largely destined for the universe these last days. The Holy Spirit, the Lord God's mind that went unsearchable until the Pentecost, filled the Lord Jesus Christ shortly after John the Baptist had baptised him in the Jordan (Matthew 3:16), accompanied him for three years as he preached the helmet of Salvation, the sword of the Spirit, the Lord God's word (Ephesians 6:17), and then accompanied Jesus Christ the King of the Universe to search all things for Christians who bow before and confess the king. He teaches us to speak the Universal Language, not speaking in words taught by human wisdom, but in words taught by him, explaining spiritual realities with spirit-taught words (1 Corinthians 2:13). The Universal language is the basis of the Christian faith. Even non-living things do have ears to hear, understand, and then obey a Universal Language speaker. Addressed through the language by the Lord Jesus Christ, for example, a storm ceased to blow (Mark 4:39), a lake let him walk on it (Matthew 14:26), a fig tree withered (Mark 11:20), and paralyses let a thirty-eight year old male pick up his mat and walk (John 5:9).

Over time, the universe evolves like the leadership of Israel did from patriarchs to prophets, from prophets to judges, and from judges to kings. The writer of Judges says that earlier when Israel had no king everyone did as they saw fit (Judges 21:25). Since the Lord Jesus Christ drank the cup of all sinners' sinfulness, and since he was crowned the King of the universe 2022 years ago, living as seen fit is not acceptable anymore. The universe is evolving towards the creation of the new heaven and the new earth, where the righteous will dwell (2 Peter 3:13). The whole universe is summoned by the Lord God to witness (Deuteronomy 30:19) as we each choose where to live after the first heaven and the first earth shall have passed away (Revelation 21:). The whole creation groans for liberation from its bondage to decay (Romans 8:21) which will be accessed only from the new heaven and the new earth.

Smoothing the Sojourn's Messiness

Destined for the unimaginably huge universe.
In Israel, I sojourned until this mess.

Salvation is from the Jews (John 4:22). The Lord God is not a God of the dead (Matthew 22:32). Once we are alive to him when still alive, we will always be when dead. Judah, Perez, Caleb, David, Mordecai, Zerubbabel, Daniel, Ezra, Nehemiah, as well as other great Jews are long buried but forever alive to the Lord God. The tribe of Judah had been in the world the most alive to the Lord God. Exquisitely and richly, the Lord God had cultivated it for Salvation. Nonetheless, the messiness of the Sanhedrin and the Lord's disciples had to be smoothed over, or Salvation would not reach the entire universe as had been intended by the Lord God. The Sanhedrin threatened to mess up with Salvation right from the beginning of the Lord's ministry, the disciples later when the Lord spoke of his departure from the sojourn.

From prison, John the Baptist heard about the deeds of the Messiah, sent his disciples to ask if the Lord had been the Messiah (Matthew 11:3), and the Lord then responded, "Go back and report to John what you hear and see (Matthew 11:4). The blind receive sight, the lame walk, those who have leprosy are cleansed, the deaf hear, the dead are raised, and the good news is proclaimed to the poor." (Matthew 11:5) Hearing of and seeing the deeds of the Messiah are what it takes to have the Christian faith. The Sanhedrin only cared about hearing of the deeds so that they could find a way to put an end to them. Google defines the Sanhedrin as the supreme council and tribunal of the Jews during postexilic times headed by a High Priest and having religious, civil and criminal jurisdiction. In their eschatology, the Messiah is a future Jewish king from the Davidic line, who is expected to be anointed with holy anointing oil and rule the Jewish people during the Messianic Age and world to come. In favour of their eschatology, they disdained hearing of and seeing the deeds of the Messiah without which the required faith for Salvation is never met. This is one way in which the Sanhedrin attempted to mess up with Salvation. Will anybody without faith in the Lord receive Salvation through grapevine communication? After the transfiguration, the Lord instructed the three apostles not to tell anyone what they had seen until he would be raised from the dead (Matthew 17:9), and he often instructed his disciples not to tell people that he was the Christ.

When the Lord had raised Lazarus from the dead, the council met and asked one another (John 11:47–48), "What are we accomplishing? Here is this man performing many signs. If we let him go on like this, everyone will believe in him, and then the Romans will come and take away both our temple and our nation." Guarding against the loss of their temple and nation to the Romans had been the Sanhedrin's added, irresistible impulsion to kill the Lord before his divine mission was accomplished. For a number of times before the

Crucifixion, they attempted to kill him. That was their second attempt to mess up with Salvation. What the Lord had told his siblings with reference to his first public appearance (John 7:6) also applied for his death: "My time is not yet here; for you any time will do." Until the Crucifixion had come and until he had drunk the cup that the Father had given him, nobody would kill him.

The Lord Jesus Christ is worthy of greater honour than Moses (Hebrews 3:3). He spiritually built the Lord God's house (Hebrews 3:3), the house which was the Jews (Hebrews 3:6), and the house for which Moses was a servant (Hebrews 3:5). The Lord told the Jews that their accuser was Moses on whom their hopes were set (John 5:45). Their hopes were not set on the Lord Jesus Christ the builder of the house, but on Moses the servant in the house. In the new play of the Lord God, all Christians are the house of the Lord God built by the Lord Jesus Christ. What a grave sin it is for Christians to set their hopes on servants in the house! Any house of the Lord God proudly said to have been built not by Jesus Christ the Builder but by a servant of the Lord God should right now be vacated. We are the house of the Lord God built by Jesus Christ the Builder. The Jewish temple was physically built by King Solomon in 957 BCE, destroyed by King Nebuchadnezzar II in 586 BCE, rebuilt in 515 BCE by Zerubbabel, expanded from 20 CE by King Herod, and destroyed by the Romans in 70 CE. The Lord God's temple that the Lord Jesus Christ built in the human heart (John 2:19), 'Destroy this temple, and I will raise it again in three days', is indestructible. "Shall I not drink the cup the Father has given me?" Intending to build indestructible temples in human hearts of Christian believers, the Lord Jesus Christ asked the epiplexis. The hopes of the Jews, however, remained set on Moses the servant in the house of the Lord God which was physically destroyed and built time after time. The most saddening fact of the millennium is that there are people today whose hopes are still set on Moses the servant. That was the third way in which the Sanhedrin attempted to mess up with Salvation. The Lord used two parables to smooth the attempt:

"No one sews a patch of unshrunk cloth on an old garment. Otherwise, the new piece will pull away from the old, making the tear worse." (Mark 2:21) Moses is compared to an antiquated torn garment, the Lord Jesus Christ to a new one. The Sanhedrin wanted to see all Jews donned in the antiquated torn garment, but the garment's shrunken power of Salvation had been sickening the Jews. Jews, Nicodemus for example, did not take off Moses the antiquated torn garment, but patched the tears with Jesus Christ the New Cloth, and then the tears became worse. Punning on the word tears makes the warning more significant: Not only holes in Moses' antiquated torn garment became increased and bigger, but the predicaments of Moses' disciples did the same and more tears were shed. The Lord Jesus Christ knew that unless he drank the cup that the Father had given him, we would not put off Moses' antiquated torn garment.

"And no one pours new wine into old wineskins. Otherwise, the wine will burst the skins, and both the wine and the wineskins will be ruined. No, they pour new wine into new wineskins." (Mark 2:22) New wine is a metaphor of the Holy Spirit explosion that is transforming the world since the Pentecost, old wineskins of Moses' disciples, and new wineskins of the Lord Jesus Christ's disciples. If the Lord Jesus Christ is to breathe the Holy Spirit on a disciple of

Moses, the disciple should first believe and be turned into the Lord's disciple, or both the Holy Spirit and the disciple will be ruined. Has any of the people whom you and I have seen in ruins been ruined by the Holy Spirit? Unfilled with the Holy Spirit, people can blaspheme against the Holy Spirit and be ruined (Matthew 12:32). On anyone ruinable by the Holy Spirit, the Lord will not breathe the Holy Spirit. If the Lord had not drunk the cup that the Father had given him Christians would like Moses' disciples abandon the Lord God when left to live up to godly maturity (Exodus 32:1): "Come, make us gods who will go before us," the Israelites instructed Aaron when they saw that Moses was so long in coming down from the mountain. Aaron made a Golden Calf for them and they worshiped it. As Christians we are led more into living up to godly maturity largely by the Holy Spirit. Our Christian leaders' role is secondary.

The Sanhedrin threatened to mess up with Salvation right from the beginning of the Lord's ministry, the disciples later when the Lord spoke of his departure from the sojourn. Apostle Peter had been Simon Bar-Jonah before the Lord had renamed him Peter, the rock on which an unwavering Christian church would be built. What a great Christian leader the Lord had foreseen in him! However, when the Lord had to leave Israel (his sojourn) for the universe (his destination) the apostle attempted to lock him away in the sojourn. The Lord then responded (Matthew 16:23), "Get behind me, Satan! You are a stumbling block to me; you do not have in mind the concerns of God, but merely human concerns." The very rock on which the Lord would build his unyielding church was a stumbling block to the Lord's divine progress. The Lord still had more work than he had done to turn Apostle Peter the loose into a hard rock. He therefore said to the apostle (John 21:18), "When you were younger, you dressed yourself and went where you wanted, but when you are old you will stretch out your hands, and someone else will dress you and lead you where you do not want to go." Foreseeing his future disciples become selfless servants of the Lord God, the Lord drank the cup that the Father had given him. In his attempt to lock the Lord away in Israel, Apostle Peter cut off Malchus' ear (John 18:10) and the Lord healed the ear and responded, "Put your sword away! Shall I not drink the cup the Father has given me?" The apostle had not understood the Lord earlier when he had said that it had been for the disciples' good that he had been going away. Until the Lord ascended to heaven, the Advocate (the Holly Spirit) would not come to them (John 16:7). He had not understood yet the paradox that the Lord's departure from Israel would be the greatest benefit to everyone.

Against the Lord's departure from Israel, the apostle spoke not only in the interests of himself and his fellow disciples, but in the interest of Israel in general. On the last day before the Ascension, the eleven disciples gathered around the Lord and asked (Acts 1:6), "Lord, are you at this time going to restore the kingdom to Israel?" Could the Lord Jesus Christ, his vision and mission be politicised, regeared towards making Israel the best economy in the world? Could they be modified to become part of politics the dirty game? About the restoration of the kingdom of Israel, he told them that it had not been for them to know the times or dates the Father had set by his own authority (Acts 1:7); then declared that they would receive power when the Advocate came on them; and they would be his witnesses in Jerusalem, and in all

Judea and Samaria, and to the ends of the earth (Acts 1:8). Finally before their very eyes, he ascended and a cloud hid him from their sight. Looking intently up into the sky as he was ascending, they thought he could forsake the Lord God's will, make Israel his destination, and then become a worldly emperor. He did not. Unless one aligns one's will with the Lord God's the Lord Jesus Christ will dishearten one. Asking the negative epiplexis "Shall I not drink the cup the Father has given me?" the Lord desired to continue smoothing over our messing up with Salvation.

In Eternal Cyclic Existence

Satan has never matched the unmatched Archangel Michael. Now his followers will follow me out of his eternal vicious cycle.

How much Satan hates being a fallen angel! He is, however, so ambitious of becoming equal with the Lord God that time after time he picks up a fight with him, lose it, and becomes a fallen angel. For countless times, Satan has been a fallen angel. He exists in an eternal vicious cycle. "How you have fallen from heaven, morning star, son of the dawn! You have been cast down to the earth, you who once laid low the nations!" Prophet Isaiah snickered at the King of Babylon (Isaiah 14:12), addressing him as Morning Star and Son of the Dawn, the original names of Satan before he had fallen from grace. The prophet saw Nimrod and Nebuchadnezzar II as incarnations, living embodiments of Satan. For countless times, Satan is a fallen angel. The first time he fell he had manipulated the natural order that the Lord God had established in heaven, got hurled down to the earth, and then got condemned as a fallen angel. Later on, he made Nimrod, the founder of Babylon, his living embodiment and commissioned the construction of the Tower of Babel against the Lord God's will. Afterwards, he made the King of Tyre

(Ezekiel 28) his living embodiment, defied the Lord God again, fell to Babylonians' forces (Ezekiel 29:18), and then got lambasted again as a fallen angel. Then he made Nebuchadnezzar II his living embodiment, built the Tower of Babel (Genesis 11), and got acclaimed as a fallen angel once more as the Lord God scattered people away from Babylon. For countless times, Satan is a fallen angel. He is caught in an eternal vicious cycle. Google defines a vicious circle as a sequence of reciprocal cause and effect in which two or more elements intensify and aggravate each other, leading inexorably to a worsening of the situation. Ambitious of becoming equal with the Lord God Satan rebelled in heaven, confronted the Archangel Michael in a war, lost the war and then became a fallen angel. His vaulting ambition to be equal with the Almighty God is the cause of his eternal problem, and his sporadic downfalls the effect of his ambition and falsified fearlessness in confronting the unequalled Archangel Michael in warfare. His adamance in not relinquishing his vaulting ambition to be God, falsified fearlessness in confronting the peerless Archangel Michael in warfare, and abhorrence for being a fallen angel keep him and his followers in the eternal vicious cycle.

"Shall I not drink the cup the Father has given me?" Knowing well that Satan had never overcome the Archangel Michael in warfare the Lord Jesus Christ asked the epiplexis. As long as an individual fought for Archangel Michael's protection, they would be protected. In drinking the cup of all sinners' sinfulness, the Lord did not cast a vote of no confidence to Archangel Michael. As the great captain, the leader of the heavenly hosts the archangel had been marvelled at when he disputed with Satan about Moses' body (Jude 1:9) and when he hurled Satan down from heaven to the earth (Revelation 12:8–9). In drinking the cup of all sinners' sinfulness, the Lord Jesus Christ augmented and complemented the Lord God's eternal virtuous cycle. Satan's eternal vicious cycle stands at the left end of the continuum of life, the Lord God's eternal virtuous cycle at the right end. The Lord Jesus Christ sanctions a deliverance of any faithful Christian from any point in Satan's eternal vicious cycle to a specified point in the Lord God's eternal virtuous cycle. Archangel Michael and the heavenly hosts he leads do the deliverance. It is a shame that Satan has never matched the unmatched Archangel Michael, and now his followers are following the Lord Jesus Christ out of his eternal vicious cycle.

The Rising Day of Selflessness

Have your sword go with the setting day of selfishness;
I am your rising day of selflessness.

The Lord Jesus Christ is the rising day of selflessness. He lived out the message of his command (John 18:11), "Put your sword away!" and his epiplexis (John 18:11), "Shall I not drink the cup the Father has given me?" He put away two all-time, great swords: The Lord God's more than twelve legions of angels (Matthew 26:53) and his I am he (John 18:6). By putting away these swords of all surpassing power, he ushered himself in as the day of selflessness, ushering out the day of selfishness. Why has the day of selfishness been too hard to usher out and why do we nostalgically often exhume it, darkening the new day? Prophet Habakkuk enquired of the Lord God why the wicked hem in the righteous, so that justice is perverted (Habakkuk 1:4). The Lord replied (Habakkuk 2:4), "See, the enemy is puffed up; his desires are not upright – but the righteous person will live by his faithfulness." The Lord God puts his laws in our minds and writes them on our hearts (Hebrews 8:10) to enhance our faith. However, our faith is too little. The day of selfishness is therefore too hard to usher out and we nostalgically often exhume it, darkening the new day? Though what is obsolete and outdated soon disappears (Hebrews 8:13), the day of selfishness haunts us, demanding that we heighten our faith in the Lord. The Lord God rewords his son's epiplexis today, "Should my son not have drunk the cup I had given him?" Our faith complements the righteousness and the salvation that the Lord gave rise to at Calvary. Through heightened faith we partake in the righteousness, and then rise with Jesus Christ the rising day of selflessness. Faithlessness somewhat proposes that the Lord's Calvary work is an otiose undertaking.

As the rising day of selflessness, the Lord reiterates without a break another epiplexis (Mark 8:36), "What shall it profit a man, if he shall gain the whole world, and lose his own soul?" There are the spirit, the soul and the body, the three human body parts. The spirit exists exclusively for the Lord God. The soul is either pure or impure, depending on its response to the bad things happening in the world. If it is pure, it gives a person individuality and humanity, a sense of self that prompts the person to take up the sword of selflessness, letting the spirit triumph. If corrupted, it impels a person to take up swords forged during the day of selfishness, letting the spirit lose. Apostle Paul's wishful thought is that the three human body parts are kept blameless at the coming of our Lord Jesus Christ (1 Thessalonians 5:23). "What shall it profit a man, if he shall gain the whole world, and lose his own soul?" the Lord reiterates this epiplexis without a break (Mark 8:36). The choice is between the soul and the whole world, between life and filthy, stinking riches. Can a corrupted soul not be vindicated freely by the Lord Jesus Christ? We are spiritually apt to opt out of filthy, stinking riches that only lead to lifeless life? The fifth (Matthew 5:7), sixth (Matthew 5:8) and seventh (Matthew 5:9) beatitudes belong to people whose souls are, among terms of purity, blameless, chaste, guiltless, honest, immaculate, impeccable, innocent, maidenly and modest. No one will have a pure soul unless they throw their sword of selfishness back to its place (Matthew 26:52) and draw the Lord Jesus Christ's sword of selflessness.

Blessed are the pure in heart, for they will see God (Matthew 5:8). As the rising day of selflessness, the Lord Jesus Christ implicitly taught his disciples to use his sword of selflessness to see the Lord God in situations where we often use swords of selfishness and see Satan. King Solomon contrasts the stirring up of anger to the churning of cream and to the twisting of the nose (Proverbs 30:33): Stirring up anger produces strife, churning cream butter, and twisting the nose blood. A slap in the face of the Lord Jesus Christ (John 18:22–23) was metaphorically not a churning of cream, but a stirring up of anger or a twisting of nose. Ironically, the Lord Jesus Christ neither punished nor killed, but gave butter to the high priest who had slapped him: "If I said something wrong, testify as to what is wrong. But if I spoke the truth, why did you strike me?" A strike on the mouth of Apostle Paul (Acts 23:1–5) was either a stirring up of anger or a twisting of nose, not a churning of cream. Did the apostle give the high priest butter straight away? No, he gave him punishment first: "God will strike you, you whitewashed wall! You sit there to judge me according to the law, yet you yourself violate the law by commanding that I be struck. The twisting of Apostle Peter's nose produced blood in seconds: He cut off Malchus ear (John 18:10)."

As the rising day of selflessness, the Lord Jesus Christ implicitly taught his disciples to use his sword of selflessness to see the Lord God in situations where we often use swords of selfishness and see Satan. "Lord, do you want us to call fire down from heaven to destroy them?" the Boanerges, James the Great and John the Apostle, wished a Samaritan village burnt like Sodom and Gomorrah for its refusal to welcome the Lord (Luke 9:52–54). The sword of selfishness they almost used is the misapplication of the Lord God's fire commonly practised by unfulfilled prophets. The Lord rebuked them, they obeyed, and then they saw the Lord God at last: They drank the cup that the Lord drank and were baptised with the baptism the Lord was baptised with. Asking the negative epiplexis, "Shall I not drink the cup the Father has given me?" the Lord knew that the world would be turned philanthropic as his fiercely obedient disciples drank the same cup.

Another sword of selfishness that John the Apostle almost used is the delusion of competing with other Christian groups, the negative attitude amongst denominational groups. The apostle reported that he had attempted to stop someone from driving out demons in the name of Jesus (Luke 9:49). Like the trinity of the Lord God, Christians everywhere should indulge in oneness, but they are billions both in number and attitude. Google says Independents within the Puritan movement were the first to define denominationalism as the belief that some or all Christian groups are legitimate churches of the same religion regardless of their distinguishing labels, beliefs and practices. The definition is based on the Scripture that says one Lord, one faith, one baptism (Ephesians 4:5). The Puritans were English Protestant Christians, primarily active in the sixteenth and eighteenth centuries CE, who claimed the Anglican Church had not distanced itself sufficiently from Catholicism and sought to purify it of Catholic practices. As a sword of selfishness the delusion of competing with other

Christian group stands against the positive Puritans' definition, and it undercuts the Lord's word that the harvest is plentiful but the workers are few, ask the Lord of harvest, therefore, to send out workers into his harvest field (Matthew 9:37–38). The Lord implicitly warns us against the delusion of competing with other Christian groups (Luke 9:50), "Whoever is not against us is for us."

Boanerges' Request Reworded

The world will at last be a philanthropic club.
If two or more soon drink from the very cup.

"You will indeed drink from my cup, but to sit at my right or left is not for me to grant. These places belong to those for whom they have been prepared by the Father," the Lord reworded the Boanerges' request (Matthew 20:23). The Lord had nicknamed James the son of Zebedee and John his brother, two of his twelve apostles, Boanerges (Mark 3:17). The word translates to *sons of thunder* in English. Of the Lord the two apostles, accompanied by their mother, had asked for the favour that in his glory he let one of them sit at his right and the other at his left. The three had identified what they had thought to be vacant positions in the Lord God's kingdom. Sitting at the Lord's right and on his left had been the two positions that they thought could soon be advertised. Not knowing what the requirements for the positions had been, they made applications. "You do not know what you are asking for," the Lord responded (Matthew 20:22). They indeed did not know what they were asking for because they had applied for unadvertised positions for which the requirements had obviously not been disclosed. Their intent to have the positions was somehow like that of Macbeth in

William Shakespeare's Macbeth: "I have no spur to prick the sides of my intent, but only vaulting ambition which o'verleaps itself and falls on th'other," (Act I Scene 7 lines 27–29). They badly desired to go to the other side, but other than their vaulting ambition they had no means to go there. Their intent, like Macbeth's, was like a steed which stands at no obstacle but jumps over. When there are no justifiable means to go to the other side vaulting ambition overleaps itself and falls on the side, said William Shakespeare. It is not a common, but a vaulting Christian faith that the Boanerges had. "You do not know what you are asking for," the Lord said, but agreed with them that the best they could ask for was to drink from his cup.

Drinking from the cup of the Lord Jesus Christ is the other side onto which only a vaulting Christian faith overleaps itself and falls. Common-faith Christians do not reach the side. Asking the negative epiplexis, "Shall I not drink the cup the Father has given me?" the Lord knew that a few Christians would outgrow common Christian faith, have vaulting Christian faith, and then drink from his cup. Drinking from the cup of the Lord Jesus Christ means to suffer or even die for him.

"You will indeed drink from my cup, but to sit at my right or left is not for me to grant. These places belong to those for whom they have been prepared by the Father," the Lord reworded the Boanerges' request (Matthew 20:23): Rather offer to drink from the Lord's cup and forget about positions. The Boanerges' vaulting faith had been out of alignment with the Lord God's will. The main requirement for drinking from the Lord's cup is an offer to be people's servant (Mark 10:43), a slave of all (Mark 10:44). The Lord aligned their vaulting faith: Standing at the Lord Jesus Christ's right and at his left-hand sides are not human services. The Lord God made angels spirits, servants flames of fire, and enthroned his son (Hebrews 1:7), and when he brought his son to the world he said (Hebrews 1:6), "Let all God's angels worship him." Standing at the Lord Jesus Christ's right and at his left-hand sides are spiritual services. An honour guard of angels always escort the Lord Jesus Christ as he empowers around the world his servants, the flames of fire.

Drinking from the cup of the Lord Jesus Christ means to suffer or even to die for him. The Lord rebuked the Boanerges for wishing a Samaritan village burnt like Sodom and Gomorrah and reworded their request to sit at his right and left sides, they obeyed him, and then drank the cup that the Lord drank, getting baptised with the baptism the Lord was baptised with: King Herod had Apostle James put to death with a sword (Acts 12:2) in 44 CE. In the late first century, the Roman emperor Domitian sent Apostle John as a prisoner to a rocky island called Patmos. There the apostle received the revelation that became the book of Revelation. A theologian called Tertullian reported that the apostle was plunged into boiling oil but miraculously escaped unscathed.

At the Name of Jesus

My Lordship by every tongue will forever be confessed;
In bowing to me, every knee enmeshed.

At the sight of the Lord Jesus Christ, impure spirits had no excuse but to fall down and confess, but at his name the unfaithfulness of Christian leaders and the faithlessness of worshipers can excuse an impure spirit from falling down and confessing. There lived exorcists at Ephesus, among whom were the seven sons of Sceva, who observed Apostle Paul driving out evil spirits and then went around exorcising (Acts 19:13), "In the name of the Jesus whom Paul preaches, I command you to come out." One evil spirit did not fall down and confess, but fought back against being driven out from its host (Acts 19:15), "Jesus I know, and Paul I know about, but who are you?" That exorcists' attempt to hijack the name of Jesus at Ephesus preceded hijacking in general, but the name of Jesus itself is unhijackable.

When impure spirits saw the Lord, they fell down before him and cried out (Mark 3:11), "You are the son of God." He had not yet drunk the cup of all sinners' sinfulness. By then, they bowed down and confessed not at his name, but at seeing him. Aware that there would be a need for all things in the universe to bow down and confess his Lordship at his name, he drank the cup. It then came to pass that at his name in heaven, on earth and under the earth every knee bows and every tongue acknowledges his Lordship to the glory of the Lord God (Philippians 2:10–11).

"Jesus, I know, and Paul I know about, but who are you?" asked an impure spirit at Ephesus. Testing spirits is as crucial to the Christian faith as scanning is to business. Christians are warned against believing spirits without testing first where they are from (1 John 4:1). They are advised to do a demon check on a spirit before they establish fellowship with it, just like impure spirits do a Holy Spirit check on Christians before they make them their hosts. Every impure spirit on earth knows that it is itself a parasite in a host that can anytime be bought at the price of the Lord Jesus Christ's blood and that shortly after the sale the host can at the name of Jesus evict it. At all costs, impure spirits on earth avoid challenging and meeting the Lord Jesus Christ and the elect of his servants whom they know about. They are afraid they can be driven out of their hosts, and then thrown back to homelessness in arid places. The impure spirit at Ephesus revealed that impure spirits only fall prostrate before the Lord Jesus Christ and the elect of his servants whom they know about: "Jesus I know, and Paul I know about, but who are you?" Apostle Paul was amongst the elect of the Lord Jesus Christ's servants whom impure spirits know about. Doing a Holy Spirit check on him, impure spirits had always found that his most famous statement (Philippians 4:13) reflected the secret behind his strengths: "I can do all things through Christ who strengthens me." His selflessness, the basic message he preached, his enormous influence on Christian theology, as well as the visionary, inspirational and self-sacrificing leadership qualities he had were not by his own might nor by his own power, but by the Spirit of the Lord God.

At the name of Jesus all things, including the angels of the Lord God, Satan and demons, bow before and confess Jesus Christ the King of the Universe. However, in his sermon 'Enter through the narrow gate' (Matthew 7:13–16) the Lord Jesus Christ distinguishes between two groups: One group travels on the narrow road and enters through the small gate. It bows down and confesses at the name of Jesus out of its own will. Not only at the name of Jesus does it fall down and confess, but it also calls upon the name of Jesus in praise and worship, as well as in praying for salvation. At the name of Jesus, the group bows down and confess on its way to life. The other group travels on the broad road and enters through the wide gate. It bows down and confesses at the name of Jesus only against its will when it is trapped or defeated. At the name of Jesus, the group bows down and confess on its way to destruction. Prophet Elisha asked the king of Israel when the Arameans had been blinded and trapped (2 Kings 6:22), "Would you kill those you have captured with your own sword or bow? Set food and water before them so that they may eat and drink and then go back to their master." The prophet spoke for the group that travels on the narrow road and enters through the small gate. The sword of the group at Spiritual Warfare is the Lord Jesus Christ: At the name of Jesus, the group's enemies are overcome. The group does not kill the enemies it traps at the name of Jesus but sets up a picnic for them and let them go back to Satan their master. In this way, the group figuratively heaps burning coals on the heads of its enemies (Romans 12:20). The figurative burning coals squeeze from the enemies the confession that Jesus Christ is Lord.

At the name of Jesus all things, including the angels of the Lord God, Satan and demons, bow before and confess Jesus Christ the King of the Universe. In style like Pharaoh's magicians, magicians fall down and confess today (Exodus 8:19), 'This is the finger of God'. When the staff that Aaron had thrown down had become a snake Pharaoh's magicians had done the same and felt that the Lord God had been their equal. The magicians continued to feel that they had an equal in the Lord God when they had performed the second and the third miracles that Aaron had performed. However, using their secret arts they did not produce the gnats that Aaron had produced out of dust, and so they figuratively fell down and confessed, 'This is the finger of God'. The production of gnats out of dust had been to the magicians a metaphor of the exploits the Lord God's finger could do. The Lord God's finger had been greater than the secret arts of Egyptian magicians. Ironically, by calling the production of gnats the Lord God's finger the magicians predicted, as if they had been the Lord God's prophets, that the Lord God's arm would cause the most disastrous plague in the world. The death of the firstborns in Egypt is indeed among the ugliest plague since the world was created. While the Lord God's finger is greater than magicians' secret arts, his arm causes the world's most calamitous epidemics.

At the name of Jesus all things, including Satan, bow before and confess Jesus Christ the King of the Universe. In style, Satan fell down and confessed at the name of Jesus when the Holy Spirit had led the Lord into the wilderness to be tempted (Luke 4). The Lord Jesus Christ's other name is the Word of God (Revelation 19:13). Using the Word of God to fight against being tempted in the wilderness, the Lord was calling upon his own name. Satan unsuccessfully tempted him for 960 hours (forty days and nights multiplied by twenty-four hours), figuratively falling down and silently confessing at the name of Jesus.

Seeing that the life of a creature is in its blood (Leviticus 17:11), the Lord God commanded the Israelites not to eat blood (Leviticus 17:12). As a creature's blood is eaten its life is as well eaten. Following a witch's specifications Gallo drank the blood of a baboon, became possessed by the spirit of the baboon, and then a witch. The nature of baboons haunted and made Gallo degenerate. How else other than at the name of Jesus could the baboon spirit be driven out of Gallo? It is hundreds of times harder to receive redemption from than to become possessed by an evil spirit. At last, a gruff voice came out of Gallo's mouth, "We are not going anywhere," as a prophet said with his hands on Gallo's head, "I cast you out in Jesus's name!" The voice's use of the plural form implied that Gallo was then possessed by a number of evil spirits additional to that of the baboon. Like the Gerasene (Mark 5:9) Gallo had come to be possessed by a legion of evil spirits. Haunted by the baboon spirit Gallo had sought deliverance from false prophets and witches. Satan does not drive Satan out but in, the Lord Jesus Christ had told teachers of the law when they had claimed that he drove out demons by Beelzebul the prince of demons (Mark 3:23). It was said that Gallo had drunk from false prophets and witches' blood of different animals, reptiles and birds, including a kangaroo's and an anaconda's.

At the name of Jesus, in heaven and on earth and under the earth, every knee should bow and every tongue acknowledge the Lord's Lordship to the Lord God's glory (Philippians 2:10–11). This Scripture mirrors three parties: Living in the Lord God's full armour, born of the Holy Spirit and accustomed to bowing and confessing Jesus Christ the King of the Universe, saints are prompted either to praise the Lord or to call on the name of Jesus for the cup of Salvation (Acts 2:21) every time they are challenged. Troublemakers, together with the spirits by which they are possessed, are the second party. Against Satan's will, they are overwhelmed to bow before and confess Jesus Christ the King of the Universe as the saints they victimise call upon the name of Jesus. This is amongst the most ideal places for the Lord God's coercive power. Far more deadly scarred of the Lord God's coercive power are Satan and his agents than Christians. Note how earnestly Legion begged the Lord Jesus Christ not to torture them (Mark 5:7–13). Legion had made the Gerasene so mentally deranged that the Gerasene could not bow before and confess the Lord Jesus Christ. Out of compassion, the Lord asked for the Lord God's coercive power to redeem the Gerasene. Knowing that they would be restless in their indigenous heavenly place, Legion asked the Lord to send them into a herd of pigs as he drove them out of the Gerasene. The third party consists of good people who are not born of the Lord God's Spirit yet, who find bowing before and confessing Jesus Christ the King of the Universe a waste of their time. These are people who believe in their own righteousness. They have no divine strength to bow before and confess the Lord or to call on his name for the cup of Salvation in times of trouble. They are their enemies' most palatable meals until they die or are triggered to be witches or Christians.

What a misuse of the name of Jesus is made by unfaithful Christian leaders and faithless worshippers! Indeed, not all of us who say to the Lord Jesus Christ 'Lord, Lord' will see the kingdom of heaven (Matthew 7:21). Gallo had been to prophets who seemed to serve the Lord God at the name of Jesus, but a legion of evil spirits killed him. At the name of Jesus in heaven, on earth and under the earth every knee bows, and every tongue acknowledges the Lord Jesus Christ's Lordship to the glory of the Lord God (Philippians 2:10–11). Gallo truly fell down and confessed at last as he fell asleep for good, but it was too late. Together with his false prophets, he was guilty of misusing the name of the Lord. The Lord will not hold guiltless anyone who misuses his name (Exodus 20:7).

"Put your sword back in its place," the Lord commanded Apostle Peter (Matthew 26:52). In the context of this command, the sword is a symbol of selfishness. Seeing that swords locked in sheaths are accessible to their owners the Lord Jesus Christ drank the cup that the Father had given him. The Lord then became a sin collector, like a garbageman. "Cast your cares on the Lord and he will sustain you," King David had prophesied back in centuries that the Lord would be a sin collector. The Lord wants us to rejoice in that our names are written in heaven, not in that impure spirits submit to us (Luke 10:20). Getting our names written in the book of life is the function of throwing our selfishness to Jesus Christ the Sin Collector. Collected by Jesus Christ the Sin Collector, our selfishness becomes unfashionable to us because he clothes us with selflessness. At the name of Jesus, our names are written in the book of life.

Quo Vadis?

So you will not be my stumbling block, Peter;
Your horizon the Father will widen wider.

Google says there is a medieval church in Rome called the Church of Quo Vadis at the sport where Apostle Peter met the Lord Jesus Christ years after the Ascension. 'Quo Vadis?' is a Latin question for the English 'Where are you going?' The medieval church throws a spotlight on to the Lord's and his disciple's footprints, brandishing the question. The Lord drank the cup that the Father had given him so that the question 'Quo Vadis?' can be brandished like a dagger. The apostle did not wish to be martyred for his faith, Google says. Fleeing from Roman authorities on the Via Appia leading out of the city he unexpectedly met the Lord Jesus Christ who had been travelling in the opposite direction. "Where are you going?" he asked the Lord. The Lord told him that he had been going to Rome to be crucified again. The apostle then realised that he could not flee from his fate. That had been shortly before the Roman Emperor Nero would blame the city's Christians for a terrible fire that had ravaged Rome. It is believed the emperor had razed the city to build a new palace, blamed it on the city's Christians, and then fatally punished them. The apostle requested to be crucified upside down, as he felt unworthy to die in the same manner as the Lord Jesus Christ.

The question is deducible from the scripture that the Lord Jesus Christ uttered before the Ascension (John 21:18), "When you were younger, you dressed yourself and went where you wanted, but when you are old you will stretch out your hands, and someone else will dress you and lead you where you do not want to go." Still enjoying the sugariness of youthful Christianity though through the Pentecost, the vision, the imprisonment and the city of Rome the Lord had done dressing him with fully-fledged Christianity, Apostle Peter tried to run away from being crucified. The apostle had already stretched out his hands, and the Lord had already dressed him up for martyrdom, but when the moment for the final self-denial drew nearer, he tried to flee from it. The Lord stopped him to inform him that the Messiah is martyred again every time any saint flees from being martyred: "I am going to Rome to be crucified again," the Lord told the apostle. That is how the Lord dressed the apostle for martyrdom again when he had fled from it. The Lord God does not rescue prospective martyrs from being martyred, for being martyred leads to a great reward in heaven. The bitter end of Christian fighters is often being martyred. Christians who fight to the bitter end flourish righteousness the most and best. That is why the Lord dressed the apostle for martyrdom again when he had fled from it.

Still enjoying the sugariness of youthful Christianity though through the Pentecost, the vision, the imprisonment and the city of Rome the Lord had done dressing him with fully-fledged Christianity, Apostle Peter tried to run away from being crucified. Was the selling process of the Gospel truth not mastered on the Pentecost? Quality prospecting had been amazingly done by the Lord God's kingdom (Acts 2:5–12). As the Holy Spirit came like the blowing of a violent wind a multi-language speaking multitude gathered together in bewilderment (Acts 2). Invitations had been subtly delivered to individuals' respective hearts. Facing the multitude turned the loose Apostle Peter into an authentic rock. The pre-approach had been nothing other than waiting in Jerusalem, not leaving the city. Waiting in Jerusalem, not leaving the city until the Pentecost called for a ten-day fasting prayer.

By enabling the disciples to speak, the somewhat universal language the Holy Spirit established an outstanding rapport that pulled the multitude close to the disciples. The Holy Spirit spoke through each disciple and interpreted to each listener in the multitude. That was the selling process' approach of the Gospel truth on the Pentecost. Apostle Peter overcame the multitude's objections before he presented the Pentecost message. "These people are not drunk as you suppose. It's only nine in the morning!" he responded when some in the multitude made fun of the Holy Spirit and the disciples (Acts 2:15). They conceived of the disciples and the Holy Spirit as drunkards and alcoholic beverages. Part of the multitude on the Pentecost asked the disciples to put away their wine (the Holy Spirit). Apostle Peter overcame the objection by linking the Pentecost with Prophet Joel's prophecy. When the multitude had seen the Pentecost as the fulfilment of the prophecy, the apostle presented the message of the day. As the apostle concluded the presentation, the multitude asked the Eleven (Acts 2:37), "Brothers, what shall we do?" How ready they were to buy the Gospel truth! The apostle closed the selling process and about three thousands of the multitude became disciples of the Lord Jesus Christ (Acts 2:41). The need to master the selling process of the Gospel truth on the Pentecost made the apostle stretch out his hands for the Lord to dress and lead him to Christian offices he had not run before.

The apostle had remained younger even after being the Lord's pupil for years. In Cornelius' house at Caesarea, he said to a large gathering of people (Acts 10:28), "You are well aware that it is against our law for a Jew to associate with or visit a Gentile." How could he expect another redress of the disassociations between the Jews and the Gentiles after the Lord Jesus Christ had already done it in Samaria (John 4)? The Lord God sent him a vision (Acts 10:11–13), accompanying it with a voice that said he should not call impure anything made pure, to get him outgrow his Christian youthfulness. King Herod had Apostle James martyred with a sword (Acts 12:2) and imprisoned the apostle (Acts 12:4). Fearing to be martyred like Apostle James, the apostle stretched out his hands, and then the Lord God's angel in style led him to Rome by taking him out of prison. He founded in Rome the Roman Catholic Church, and he is counted as the first bishop of Rome–the pope.

Fleeing from his own crucifixion, the apostle was stopped and informed by the Lord, "I am going to Rome to be crucified again." The apostle then realised that he could not flee from his fate. Is it not fallacious that we are helpless in the face of fate? The apostle had written his own fate: He had made two declarations, that even if all his fellow disciples fell away on account of the Lord he never would (Matthew 26:33) and that even if he had to die with the Lord he would not disown him (Matthew 26:35). Unlike iron that can be heated and then bent, fate stands the tests of all things. Against his first declaration, the apostle disowned the Lord thrice before the rooster crowed but was reinstated; and against the second he tried to flee from his crucifixion but was gently urged to go back for it. The Lord drank the cup that the Father had given him so that whoever has faith to engrave their fate in him forever can do so.

Quo Vadis Church throws a spotlight on to the Lord's and his disciple's footprints, brandishing like a dagger the question 'Where are you going?' The Lord Jesus Christ nods his approval to those who stretch out their hands, signalling that they want him to dress them and lead them where they do not want to go.

Made in the USA
Monee, IL
03 May 2026

49438362R00036